I0813149

History of the Titanic

Building the Titanic

by Julie Murray

Dash!
LEVELED READERS
An Imprint of Abdo Zoom • abdobooks.com

Level 1 – Beginning
Short and simple sentences with familiar words or patterns for children who are beginning to understand how letters and sounds go together.

Level 2 – Emerging
Longer words and sentences with more complex language patterns for readers who are practicing common words and letter sounds.

Level 3 – Transitional
More developed language and vocabulary for readers who are becoming more independent.

abdobooks.com

Published by Abdo Zoom, a division of ABDO, PO Box 398166, Minneapolis, Minnesota 55439.
Copyright © 2025 by Abdo Consulting Group, Inc. International copyrights reserved in all countries. No part of this book may be reproduced in any form without written permission from the publisher. Dash!™ is a trademark and logo of Abdo Zoom.

Printed in the United States of America, North Mankato, Minnesota.
102024
012025

Photo Credits: Alamy, AP Images, Getty Images, Shutterstock
Production Contributors: Kenny Abdo, Jennie Forsberg, Grace Hansen, John Hansen
Design Contributors: Candice Keimig, Neil Klinepier

Library of Congress Control Number: 2024936555

Publisher's Cataloging in Publication Data

Names: Murray, Julie, author.
Title: Building the Titanic / by Julie Murray
Description: Minneapolis, Minnesota : Abdo Zoom, 2025 | Series: History of the Titanic | Includes online resources and index.
Identifiers: ISBN 9781098287221 (lib. bdg.) | ISBN 9781098287924 (ebook) | ISBN 9781098288273 (Read-to-me ebook)
Subjects: LCSH: Shipbuilding--Juvenile literature. | Ships--Welding--Juvenile literature. | Vessels (Ships)--Juvenile literature. | Historic ships--Juvenile literature. | Titanic (Steamship)--Juvenile literature.
Classification: DDC 910.9163--dc23

Table of Contents

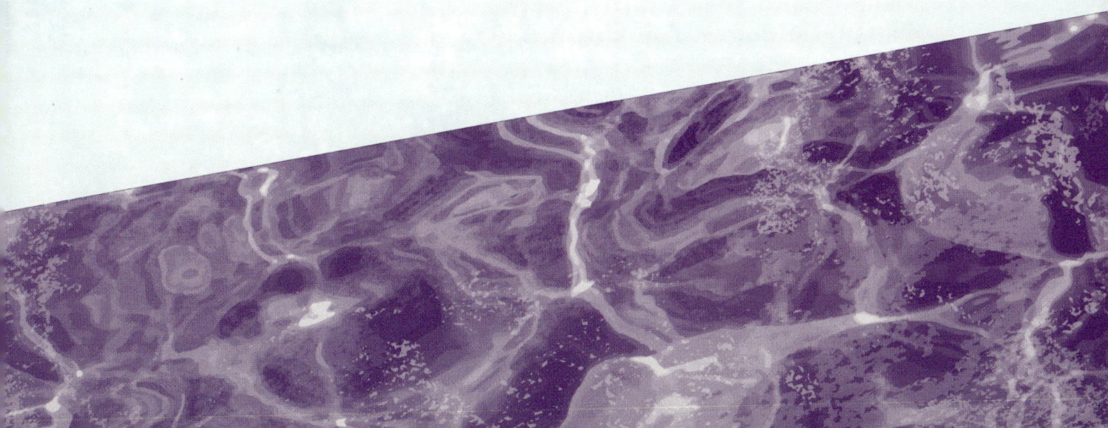

Building the Titanic

The **RMS** *Titanic* was the biggest ship of its time. It took around 3,000 workers three years to build the ocean liner.

From Beginning to End

Construction began on March 31, 1909. The *Titanic* was built in a **shipyard** in Belfast, Ireland.

The ship's **keel** and **frame** were built first. Curved steel beams created the shape of the ship.

OLYMPIC

Steel plates were attached to create the **hull**. More than three million **rivets** were used!

WHEEL HOUSE
3rd CLASS PROMENADE
CLOSED BULKH
3rd CLASS
OPEN SPACE
3rd CLASS STAIRCASE
STAIRS
TO
DECK
HATCH
WATER LINE
SQUASH RACQUET COURT
MOTOR CARS
SPIRAL STAIRCASE
WATER TIGHT BULKHEAD
BAGGAGE CARGO ETC
BULKHEAD
DOUBLE

There were 16 compartments in the ship's **hull**. The compartments had watertight doors. The doors could be closed to contain a leak.

The *Titanic* required three large engines. They were fueled by steam from burning coal.

The ship had four **smokestacks**. Only three worked. The fourth stack was meant to make the ship look grander.

The *Titanic's* interior was the last to be finished. It included a grand staircase, restaurants, and 840 guest bedrooms.

Building was complete on March 31, 1912. The *Titanic* was 883 feet (269 m) long. It stood 175 feet (53 m) tall.

More Facts

- It cost about $7.5 million to build the *Titanic*. Today, it would cost $400 million to build the ship.

- Eight workers died during the ship's construction. Two hundred and forty-six were injured.

- The *Titanic* had a pool, barber shop, squash courts, a gymnasium, and much more.

Glossary

frame - a structure made of parts that are joined together and that supports a larger object.

hull - the rigid frame and outer shell of a ship.

keel - a long piece of wood or metal that runs down the length of the bottom of a boat or ship. The keel makes a boat or ship stable in the water.

rivet - a metal bolt that pins metal plates or other objects together.

RMS - short for Royal Mail Ship.

shipyard - a place where ships are built or repaired.

smokestack - a tall chimney.

Index

Online Resources

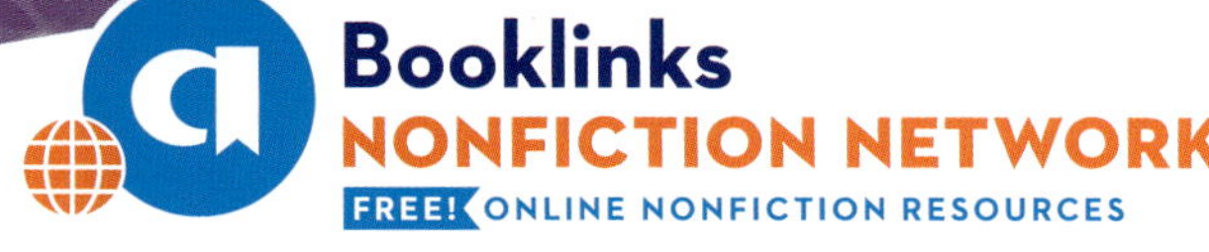

To learn more about building the *Titanic*, please visit **abdobooklinks.com** or scan this QR code. These links are routinely monitored and updated to provide the most current information available.